THINKING OF SANTORINI:
POEMS 1974–2015

Andy Godfrey

THINKING OF SANTORINI:
POEMS 1974 – 2015

Vanguard Press

VANGUARD PAPERBACK

A CIP catalogue record for this title is
available from the British Library.

ISBN 978 1 78465 161 9

Vanguard Press is an imprint of
Pegasus Elliot MacKenzie Publishers Ltd.
www.pegasuspublishers.com

First Published in 2016

Vanguard Press
Sheraton House Castle Park
Cambridge England

Printed & Bound in Great Britain

For Claudi (White Cloud) – and others

Acknowledgements

Many thanks to Pegasus, in particular Andrew Smith and Suzanne Mulvey, for offering me the opportunity to appear in print; also, to all the team there who worked so hard on this book.
To those whose belief in me as a poet gave me so much inspiration and encouragement over the years – thank you.

CONTENTS

Earlier Work: 1974 – 1986

Australian Sunrise

A bright bar –
molten metal
divides sky and land.
Spilling upwards light
floods the moleskin
earth revealing shapes
of silver waters great
flat running wolf
spread over the old ground
like a worn-out skin.
Atomic eye
eases over the rim
subtly infecting
brilliantly
subduing vitality
coming to rest
on a pale platter.

12.8.74

Rainbows towards Adelaide

In the yellowing light
two rainbows sprout
from folded hills
pressing their soft bars
into a lead sky

27.8.74

Sydneysiders

I

They sit there the ladies
In George St., next to Gowings,
Turning people's lives
This way and that
Hoping for some illumination
On a Monday before Christmas.

II

A crack divides the hum
Always like this
The tray that drops
As people sit and stare
And the smell of coffee sharpens
In the corner of Menswear.

III

A late tea
Orange Chiffon
Red hibiscus on a lace cloth
And some past baritone winding
                         slowly
Around the airy rooms
Over Castlereagh Street
Emptying of shoppers.

IV

Are they Poles I wonder
Who sit in threes
Across a chess-board
In the park
And talk into an open
                         space
With red flowers as their only
                         audience?

21 Dec. 81

Morning Tea at Riza's

She serves tea to you
As the Japanese serve tea:
It becomes a sacrament
Incongruous in its place
In the café with
      the torn floor-boards
Where the flies move lazily
      in and out.

The Jazz Garter

The second-hand hang there
Shrouds of past wearers
While the walkers glide by
Out of step with Bing
They shuffle and peer
At their ghostlier counterparts.

22 Dec. 81

King George's Garden

Amphitheatre of flowers
Each row a variation;
The grey bird that struts
Endlessly turning the moist earth,
As the unresisting bowl
Receives its morning sounds.

Angel Arcade

The honey man has departed
Taking his Royal Jelly with him
The golden jars
Captives of long, hot summers
Have taken something away
From the Angel Arcade.

Temple Court: 11 a.m.

This is the hour when
The solicitors are abroad
Purveyors of justice
A keen wind ruffles
The tightly rolled bundles
Of living details under each arm.

On the 14th. floor

On the 14th. floor
A girl in a lilac shift
Discusses the hopeless case
Her papers an untidy heap.

An elderly pair
Of ladies from David Jones
Face an opaque view
Their hands explode with
Endless stories.

The barrister nods and smiles
In wreaths of smoke
His wig sits mute
Guarding a fat file.

The Qantas Pilot

A man pursued
By the brutal honesty of a
                    revelation,
He stumbles upon a tray
Indiscriminately feeding
    Upon Big Macs
Or David Jones' Specials.

23 Dec. 81

'Aquatic World', Waterloo

Ceaseless movement
A ribbon of snake
Flicks through the bubbling blue;
Seahorses gyrate
Cheeks rise and fall
As they draw head tight to neck
And meditate.
The crab
Sole spectator of its own
                    reflection
Stands poised, one leg aloft;
While the goldfish
Shoot fiery bodies
Through crowded tanks.

Shepherds

Kitty and Marie
Wheeling trolleys
They awkwardly push them
Across the road
Returning the lost sheep
To their particular supermarkets.

24 Dec. 81

Sydney Hospital

I saw a chimney belching smoke
Away into the patch of blue;
A stark reminder that
Even on Christmas afternoon
The incinerators are busy.

25 Dec. 81

Christmas Tree

The Christmas tree
Stands silently
Its branches decked with
                    tinsel
A mute witness
Of all the night's happenings
It waits
As the cool-throated birds
Warble and cry –
Their notes falling
Into a circle of light –
And a single dog barks.

Ten to six

It is not usual
That I am awake
To see the wetness
Of the world
Arcs of birds
Trying out the pale amphitheatre
Of an apricot sky
That turns so quickly
Into the usual day.

N.S.W.G.R. Booking Hall

Its warmth belies
The sombre light
That filters through
          stained-glass windows
A couple converse
The rise and fall
Forming a lullaby
To the man that sleeps
Stretched on a seat.
Flaming rose and purple hill
Become a background
Against which
     the ticket clerks
Ply their trade.

Boxing Day Morning

Coasting down William Street
The warm sun in my face
Past the women who lean and wait
(Until they have lost the notion
Of what they are waiting for)
And into more sunshine
And shadows spilt
From the green expanse
Of Rushcutters Park
On a Boxing Day Morning.

26 Dec. 81

The Christmas Tree

Decorated
Celebrated
It stands
In the place of honour
A fabulous guest
Its past glittering
From tinselled boughs
That hold the god
High to his death.

28 Dec. 81

Prayer Mat

On crinkled plush
Two dancers dance
A musician's hand
Is raised. Wild strains
Create a turbid wall
Of sound. Feet
That tread measures
Embroidered features
Blurred through dry-cleaning.

13.4.82

Sunset near Canberra

Setting sun
that gilds the white grasses
casts a pink shadow
over the mountain's shoulder.
Clear air
that brings a bird's call
to round and sweeten
in the ear.

Sydney, 3.1.82

Kendall Country

The tree that Henry sat under
leans towards an obscured valley.
A forgotten mill. Inhabitants
will not forget. They lean
across a grocery counter
eager to share their celebration
and information
culled over the years.
'He would've had a drink
with us, y'know. The minds
of poets – well, they need the wine!'
Like bellbirds
their high laughs ring out
over the brooding hillsides.

20.1.82

For Russ, 25 Jan. 1986

In the House of the Dying Man

And then it was
That living seemed to partake
Of that which had been reserved
For the dead.

Women's voices with their rise and fall
Endless litany of detail
Small palliative measures
A temporary occupation –
Inheritors of a time now lost
When the mind's mirrors
Glittered with a man's world-view
Enlarging our vision.

Oh endless toil –
No soothing ritual for the departing
But hourly combat against
The heralded decay of a private empire
An ever–shrinking compass
The single cell.

A Wednesday in Forster

Today I've entertained an electrician
apologised to a neighbour
complained to an agent
bought a passion-fruit cream sponge
exchanged a pot
drunk coffee in a gift shop
cycled to Burgess Beach
collected three snappers
grilled three blade steaks
altered two tank-tops
re-vacuumed black dust
scrubbed a bikini
apportioned a banana
chased two kids off my bed
cooled down a room
& finished reading Orlando —

22.1.81
(final changes, 16.11.94)

Later Poems: 1991 – 2015

Grandmother

Always the knitting
Under and over our lives
But when did you become
A wandering stitch by your needles
Slipped off? You die
And are born for me
In my hot land.
Stitch lost too late
Perhaps falling as the other dangles
Your double
In that hellish time when
The eye dulled and the ear thickened
Against the dark.
Like the words of strangers,
The unemployed in these impatient hands.

Hamburg, 20.2.91

(After the rediscovery of Paul Klee's *The Golden Fish*)

The Magic Fish

Twenty years and you hadn't swum.

Icon of gold
sharp-finned
Pink points
in the velvet possibilities
of past time.
Unclear Nature embraced
that other determination
in a black and yellow skin,
gathered me, an uncertain swimmer,
into the mind's Australias.

Motionless collision,
Möbius strip
of inarticulated boundaries
traced by the crossings of fish.

Hamburg, 8.3.91

Hagenbeck's Zoo

G.C. Hagenbeck
founder of the Firm,
knew what was good.
Stellingen calmed us
gave the unusual
such cosy distance.

European skins
faded, resigned,
numb in the waiting
Let's order hopelessness,
perhaps provide the proper space?

Blackbird with dinosaur –
Scale is important.
After all, isn't it always the era
for measuring yourself
against what others aren't?

Indian, African,
Lion and Bear
stand in bronze time
with Elephants
whose trunks lift lamps
lift the single bird's song
lonely and free
under a pale moon.

Hamburg, 25.3.91

Johannisbeeren

yes, alright, we deify them,
these moments when all seems held in marvellous
accord – Joyce's 'moments of epiphany' – but
isn't there good reason to? After the fury, mess
of another Tripoli, Bagdad, at last I'm here again, with you.
How much the painters loved this scene!
The women sit around the table under trees,
late afternoon, their dappled, solid bodies; faces
half-shaded – phrases, half-said words
hands moving gentle through heaps of bright fruit,
practised fingers catching stray rolling berries –
Johannisbeeren: pierced by the slanting sun
red-gold among the dusky leaves they hang,
little translucent globes. You rightly say we can't
see from outside in – the lived experience;
all this I know, and yet –

Hamburg. 8.7.93

Johannisbeeren: red currants

Sonnet in Harry's Voice

We want to have back the old times
when everything walked in special ways.
Two old people on their farm:
the cows are in
everything is done
and you are coming home.
All these problems are outside;
they are not inside.
But this was for you, not for me.
I lived this life
as everybody lived it,
and what you
would call in English 'love'
was for me a side effect.

Hamburg, 16.9.93

Schaliß 1,0 km

Schaliß 1,0 km
Swimming in the lake

Schaliß 1,0 km (für Claudia)

It was the afternoon the geese flew south
westwards into a sinking sun
surprised we heard their cries
wingbeats even stroking, ribboning pearl
the sharp blue air. A lone flyer: "come on,
the other way", you called;
stones leaping the still water
lapped with your eyes
mouth soft, serious pleasure
asking why so sad:
only that I'm here gazing out
at last across the lakes
of Mecklenburg-Vorpommern.

17.11.93 (Buß u. Bettag)

Swimming in the lake (for Cloud)

Flying the autobahn's cloudless heat
points shimmer blue in the grasses
June: the Raps is late this year,
drumming yellow the fields
cadmium to chrome. And Zarrentin's under our wheels
windows open to earth, hay-smell, the flies
that lovingly circle our heads, bodies without desire
the waters clasp us until we
warming sharp silver cleaving sun's passion
skin on skin, as dragonflies lightly
observing ourselves take
this paradise – end of the world; day
sweet as eelflesh
eaten at Schaalsee, on the wharf,
feet hanging loose
in the lake's cool brown.

Hamburg, 25.6.94

Paradise lost

At five o'clock I heard the crows: harsh cries
they split the air
My bags were packed, but still
I stood and lingered in the hall
And then it seemed I heard a voice
speak from across the years:
"Please leave the place as it was found.
All breakages must be replaced." But
does this mean those things worn down
by sadness, anger and despair? The things
through which love's constancie
at last from hope departs?

16.7.94

Dinner party

the fare of the rich
is too rich for me –
I long then for a simple thing –
the wind on my face
treesmell damp, shaking
light through their leaves
sparkling the grass, Heußweg
mid-afternoon. Coming home
I stay in my shirt, eat an egg –
sunflowers brim yellow my eye
thin me out to bright sleep,
and a waking into the dark –

Hamburg, 10.9.94

1. thinking of Santorini

thought catches fire
as colour drowns the eye
and senses dream the imaged
long-ago
of bodies, harbours, the incurious gaze
of stone, a time that shards the will
laid bare such substance as we had,
of Santorinis
that we never knew

HH/Kreta
11.4.95/18.4.95

2. Kreta

a plain we drove
where nothing dies or moves
read history's cipher
in each twisted sign to
where the wild anemone grows
on Omalos

and straight we fell
stone-winding into sheeted seas
easy as birds
with every mountain's fall
springing sun's slanting
cut of the wave

then how we held the lustred groves
of afternoon, the poppied split
of arid soil, women's dark labours
in their villaged quiet
turned us toward starred silence,
break of the lifted foam
in unskeined sleep

Kreta/HH
17.4.95/25.4.95

say goodbye to them these cliffs

say goodbye to them these cliffs
let the spool of my thoughts unwind
as lightplay on water
larkhigh
climb of a shouldered sun
gullplaint
& tug of a grass-smell wind
sloped to the gorsefall crash
of rocks slabbed wet
& Lamledra crouched
in a foxgloved dark
the sacred sites of the heart –

Gorran H. 30.5.95/HH 13.6.95

Kayaking (for Cloud)

Kayaking

the fields lie harvested
smooth flick of paddles
        light across the lake
pooled banks of cloud shift
           slowing to our rhythm

The Müritz

then the Müritz – better than
imagined Imagining
        those Maori warriors
ploughing each furrow
driving each fury
cresting with passions
        their higher waves

Recovery

I see you with that butterfly you lifted
gently off the Kölpinsee
bending low, cupped hands, warm breath
a rayed afternoon
         into which she floats
         under which I lie
exhausted on the grass

Plauer crossing

windsong slapping
crisscross of dark waters
when where to fix a middle-point
         became our only thought –
& at the camp it was so hot
You tried to roll me, laughing,
& we slipped smooth as seals
         beneath our boats

At Zielow

the serious girl
who does not think she is
        good-looking
lies and reads philosophy
by the lake
        there we build fires
with rotting boughs

FKK

in FKK there's still no space
familial only
        differently generationed
Those times I caught
their looks, your eyes
having read Yevtushenko,
finding it noone's fault
quailed at such distances
those days
        I was my own best friend

Mirow, 24.7.95/HH, 23.8.95

Schloß (Klink)

a headless woman
in the burning sun she sits
        amongst the grass
where tourists crunch
        on shattered glass & gape
at sags of wallpaper in grimy rooms
No fairytale this story
overall remains the same
where delicate spires
        raise slanted whorls
cry demolition by neglect

        Mirow, 24.7.95/HH,23.8.95

Roll back the years
return to me
the undivided power
of youth
to live anew

Recall lost time
those fallow years
spent wandering
in aimless doubt
anneal my purpose
so to strike

Drive a true furrow
shape work of hand and mind
oh heal each rift
to spring my trap
of bodied soul

For Wolf, 14 November 1996

Circus lion (for Dee)

circus lion
shaggy lion
have you any tricks?
you tricked yourself
out to please
lost yourself
in their hands

shaggy lion
circus lion
you gave yourself away
lived their lives
not your own
thought you needed
what they did

circus lion
shabby lion
can't you make us laugh?
how you clowned
your dream not ours
confused the real
became your cage

HH, 11.9.96/Mykonos, 1.7.97/Skiathos, 6.7.97

Delfi

only the swallows have stayed
unconcerned and at home
with these broken stones
columns marked time not ours
long gone
guides that re-tell
the old stories
of what we should look for
alone
the trees in silence offer their shade
(rustle of water, slither of lizard)
give temporary shelter
from questions that burn
under the blinding sun

Delfi, 26.6.97/Paros, 29.6.97

Myth

once again we were waiting
for the ship that didn't arrive
you fell asleep on the ground
amongst the cigarette butts
we didn't speak
it was one of those times
noone spoke
peering into the dark
we were only waiting
for this moment to pass
for the ship to come
and release us

Mykonos/Skiathos, 2.7.97

Albatross (on the loss of the GDR) (for Cloud)

a bird there was
once a bird
flew far and wide
through ev'ry storm
believing itself free
betrayed

a land there was
once a land
visioned brave
clipt certain wings
stripped given truths
itself betrayed

never having lived your truth
we are the poorer
we who cannot free ourselves
from your weight
around our necks

Paralia Ag. Anas, 26.6.97/Paros, 29.6.97/Skiathos, 6.7.97

Fairy stories

1. Beauty in the waking

how little the storytellers told us
of that propitious moment: of her rising fears
mounting to brush the foreign lips,
and sly conceit that swelled his gaze,
a trust that left no place for doubt;
for was he not the One, true scaler
of thorny cage and mossy wall
bound in their hundred-year silence?
all this she must have known
but in the waking
found that she'd lose: how certainty's sweet sleep
capped by the summits of untested dream,
faced with this newest of cold dawns,
slid from her fearful clasp.

2. An early version of Hitchcock

in a way it's an early version of Hitchcock
the six swans
you wonder if they'll make it in time
and she on her way to the stake
in a tumbril, endlessly stitching the shirts
that would free them
and nearer to speaking
her mind, the crowd so unprepared
she hesitates to hurt
disturb their image of the gentle girl
mute with her nettles –
and it would never do
to turn into harpy;
she spoke her truth, such empty silence,
and watched them as they turned away;
it was quite late, and they were tired.

Hamburg, 1.8.96/20.1.97/4.4.98

Skiathos, 3rd. of July (for Cloud, at her request)

first-light sound
laps naked our sleep:
cock-crow, purr of a myriad bees,
the swifts' sharp cries
piercing each dawn;
now dog-bark, gruff note
grumble of horse;
what joy then tumbling out
with all our harmonies
into the sun's single blast.

being back (for Hon)

each day will be better
being back
we'll begin to forget the small rituals
so strangely housed in our bodies
honey, shared fruits, water,
drinking-in of the sun, seas
hours at Mandraki,
desiring to sleep after the shower before
venturing freshly to greet,
a leap in the pulse, cool vitality
tasting the smell of crisp fish
that rabbit we relished
taking each day
up on the roof, with the flickering candle
a cig. and retsina
under the cluster of stars

HH, 13.7.97

Suicide

he stumbles on
your new-found friend
through endless dark, a Danish forest,
crying your name, half falls against
the hanging, stiffening legs,
dropping to weep among the shrivelling leaves.
Bereft.
I find them too easy by far these phrases
to perhaps explain away your death.
At twenty-nine you were no child;
by what paths did you travel
to that tree you chose
out of your daily loneliness?
for me the paradox is this:
you did not die alone;
we all had a hand in it

28th September 1998;
On hearing about the death of a student who hung herself in a
Danish forest, while holidaying there.

For Claudi – who gave me such images
of her Zoo. Then.

In the East

In the east
we felt close to our heroes:
at least there was a park
(Clara Zetkin Park)
or a street – that was something –
even if they were now
like shucked-off clothes, old hat,
crumbly brickwork, a sign.

And the Monument – blackened granite,
a man
aged in silence, unseeing –
verarscht – as the old tigers
that wait without hope
behind their rusted bars.

Leipzig, 29.3.01

Russian Denkmal

Stifling gloom glowing dark
suspended
hanging swaddled in chants
spiralling upwards –
Are they singing? – No, it's this CD –
And, no cameras please! – Silence, respectful,
snagged by a sob, headscarved,
unbreathable; the woman's tears
panelled ikons in time
against which her three candles
are wavering
here and now. – Spassibo. Pozhujsta!

Spassibo: Thank you.
Pozhujsta: You're welcome!

Leipzig, 29.3.01

Seen from the train

and to long for the freedom
of the girl who climbs upon the sandpile
unthinking
in the late afternoon

Leipzig – Wittenberge, 29.3.01

Lilac Tree

Today they killed
the best part of you –
I played you a requiem,
wept for such beauty
I had known
outside my window.
Tonight I play you
Bocelli – hope –
his voice rises blindly
as you will raise your face
to tomorrow's sun.

Eimsbüttel, 8.8.2005

The Crows

The cries of crows,
Neubrandenburg,
had accompanied us then
through flakes of snow – do you remember?
Had flooded the Hof
with their echoes.
An echo of these, a single crow
seen here
alone in Stralsund –
and again my ear is filled
with their cries.

On the train to Bad Banzin
5.7.2008

Hof: inner courtyard

Blackbirds

A blackbird sings the day awake
Tiny crystals of sound
Falling into the dark Hof.

By day they hop, are all intent
Spying worms in the juicy grass.
Even when I'm old
There'll always be blackbirds.

4.15 a.m., 11.7.2009

A Thursday in Hamburg

Standing at the bus stop
with a head full of Yeats & a pocket full of Centrelink
it's rained in the night, is steamy,
and on the short grass, blackbirds

there's the usual Hinweis für Fahrgäste
at the Rathausmarkt
where the swans are cleaning themselves
and Touris are wandering hin und her

Hinweis für Fahrgäste: 'advice for passengers' – on the bus
Touris: slang for tourists
Hin und her: to and fro – they wander in front of buses

Hamburg, 10,11.6/5.7.10

Chiaroscuro

this is the time of shadows
of light and dark
and edges – sharp – that one bumped into
or, unnoticed, a shape
they invaded the pictures
How weren't they seen before?
They were surely there
lying across one's life – waiting
not blinded by colours
but perhaps a jacket
of a certain green
that gets itself noticed
at a table
in the glare of an autumn sun

HH/23,24.9.15